Witness History Series

CHINA SINCE 1945

Stewart Ross

The Bookwright Press
New York

1989

Titles in this series

China since 1945
The Origins of World War I
The Russian Revolution
The Third Reich

First published in the
United States in 1989 by
The Bookwright Press
387 Park Avenue South
New York, NY 10016

First published in 1988 by
Wayland (Publishers) Ltd
61 Western Road, Hove
East Sussex BN3 1JD, England

Library of Congress Cataloging-in-Publication Data
Ross, Stewart.
    China since 1945 / by Stewart Ross.
        p.   cm.
    Bibliography: p.
    Includes index.
    Summary: Discusses the history of China
from Mao's Communist takeover in 1945,
through the Great Leap Forward and the
Cultural Revolution, to the changes that have
taken place since the death of Mao.
    ISBN 0–531–18220–7
    1. Communism – China – History – Juvenile
literature.
    2. China – Politics and government – 1945–
1949 – Juvenile literature.   3. China – Politics
and government – 1949 – Juvenile literature.
[1. Communism – China – History.   2. China –
Politics and government – 1945–1949.   3. China
– Politics and government – 1949–   4. China –
History – 1949 –]
I. Title.
HX418.5.R67   1989
335.43'45'09 – dc19   87–37519
                                             CIP
                                             AC

Typeset by Kalligraphics Limited, Redhill, Surrey
Printed and bound by Sagdos, S.p.A., Milan

Chinese names

Since 1972 Chinese names have been translated
using the Pinyin system. This book uses Pinyin,
except where a name appears in a quotation in
the old Wade-Giles translation. Here are some of
the more widely used names according to both
systems:

Old (Wade-Giles)	New (Pinyin)
Chiang Kai-shek	Jiang Jieshi
Chiang Ching	Jiang Qing
Chou En-lai	Zhou Enlai
Chu-teh	Zhu De
Hua Kuo-feng	Hua Guofeng
Lin Piao	Lin Biao
Liu Shao-chi	Liu Shaoqi
Mao Tse-tung	Mao Zedong
Peng Te-huai	Peng Dehuai
Teng Hsiao-ping	Deng Xiaoping
Canton	Guangzhou
Kuomintang	Guomindang
Nanking	Nanjing
Peking	Beijing
Shantung	Shandong
Shensi	Shaanxi
Yangtze	Chang Jiang
Yenan	Yanan

Abbreviations

The following well-known abbreviations have
been used in the text:

GMD (KMT)	Guomindang (Kuomintang)
CCP	Chinese Communist Party
USSR	Union of Soviet Socialist Republics (Russia)
PLA	People's Liberation Army

55543

Cover illustration: A poster published
during the Cultural Revolution entitled
"Long Live Chairman Mao."

Contents

The Chinese Empire

IN 1900 ABOUT ONE quarter of the world's population lived in China. Although the huge Chinese Empire covered an area almost the size of Europe including European USSR, only about one-eighth of the land was fertile, and most of the population was crowded into the east of the country near the great Yellow and Chang Jiang rivers. To the north stretched the barren flat lands of the Gobi desert, while farther west rose the sharp, inhospitable peaks of the Himalayan mountains. Within this vast country there was a broad range of cultures, languages, customs and religions.

Chinese civilization stretched back over at least 3,000 years. The first Chinese Emperor began his rule in 221 BC. Not only were the emperors the political rulers of China but they also claimed to hold "Heaven's Mandate" to rule. They were seen as semi-religious figures. When things went badly for a dynasty or there was a natural disaster such as a flood (the shallow, heavily silted Yellow River was frequently flooded), it could be seen as a sign that a

China in about 1900. Because of its great size and power, China regarded all neighbors as "barbarians," building the Great Wall in 221 BC along its northern frontier to keep invaders out. In the nineteenth century this attitude made it very difficult for the Chinese to accept that the West might have anything valuable to offer them.

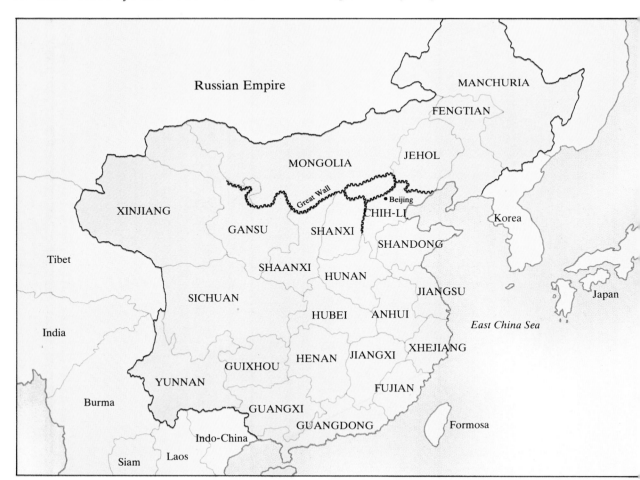

The Great Wall of China.

dynasty had lost Heaven's Mandate, and revolts might occur.

The last dynasty to seize power was the tough northerners, known as the Manchu, in the middle of the seventeenth century. The Chinese regarded them as foreigners because they came from the remote area of Manchuria. Their empire was held together by a chain of command that ran from the Emperor, through his national council and prefects, to district and sub-district governors. Below them groups of villages made up associations, whose chiefs were the key link between central and local government. Since the journey between Beijing and Shanghai took twenty-three days, it is easy to imagine how difficult it was for the Manchu emperors to keep close control of the more distant provinces. Law and order was reinforced by the philosophy of Taoism, which emphasized harmony, peace and respect for authority, and by the great moral system of Confucianism, which was adopted by the educated, ruling classes.

Through the centuries the cultural and scientific achievements of the Chinese had been immense, including the invention of paper, printing and gunpowder, and the creation of the most exquisite paintings, carvings, poetry and architecture. Nevertheless, the great majority of the population still lived in dire poverty. Moreover, complacency had replaced creativity in the ruling classes, and the powerful modern scientific and technological innovations of the West were largely ignored. To the Chinese, in fact, Westerners were merely "barbarians."

Revolution and disintegration

For centuries the Western nations were permitted only limited trade with China. In the nineteenth century, however, the Western traders introduced the Chinese to opium, although China had manufactured a little opium for medicinal purposes. When the Chinese government objected to this trade, the Westerners used their military strength to get their way. By 1910 not only had Japan and the European nations forced the Chinese to trade on their terms but they had also seized large areas of the Chinese Empire: Korea, Indochina, Burma, Formosa and much of eastern Manchuria being some of the most important.

Besides being bullied by the more technologically advanced nations, the Manchu government faced mounting trouble at home. Throughout the nineteenth century the population of China continued to rise. As it did so, there was less and less land for the peasants. As taxes and rents became more difficult to bear, hostility against landlords and the government mounted. After

the bloody Taiping Rebellion of 1851–64, in which perhaps 40 million people died, there were some attempts at reform. These came to nothing, however, and when the old Empress Tzu Hei died in 1908 leaving the throne to a 3-year-old child, it was clear that the end of the Manchu dynasty was near.

The central character of the revolution of 1911 was a Westernized Christian, Dr. Sun Yatsen. Sun Yatsen, who was proclaimed President of China on January 1, 1912, led the Guomindang (GMD) party, whose principles were nationalism, democracy and people's livelihood (which he later compared with socialism). But, Sun Yatsen was not able to control the forces he had brought into being, and in 1912 an ex-imperial general, Yun Shikai, assumed the presidency. When he died in 1916 the country fell under

Prisoners being led away for execution during the 1911 revolution. Beheading with a sword was a traditional method of execution in China.

Starving peasants. Peasant unrest more than any other factor led to the fall of the Manchu dynasty. But until 1949 subsequent governments seemed unwilling or unable to do anything about the suffering of the masses.

the control of "warlords," powerful local generals who established themselves as petty kings in different parts of the country.

After Sun Yatsen's death in 1925, leadership of the GMD passed to the soldier, Jiang Jieshi. In 1928 Jiang, who seemed to care little for Sun Yatsen's original principles, declared himself ruler of China, although he never controlled the whole country. Years of civil war and disturbance had made the conditions of the peasants even worse than before. For the workers in the new industrial areas along the eastern seaboard, such as Shanghai, things were no better. Child labor was common, wages pitiful, and conditions of work intolerable. In the eyes of the ordinary Chinese citizen, peasant or factory hand, only one group seemed to have their true interests at heart, and they were the Communists.

War

When in 1917 Lenin and the Bolshevik Communist Party seized power in Russia, a small group of Chinese intellectuals took great heart and began to call for a Communist revolution in China. The Chinese Communist Party (CCP) was founded in July 1921 by Professor Li Dazhao and Chen Duxiu. Mao Zedong, who was later to become the famous Communist leader, was present at the meeting.

At first the CCP and the GMD of Dr. Sun Yatsen worked together, with Russian help, forming a United Front in 1923. Jiang Jieshi, however, hated the Communists and in 1927 he broke with the United Front, ordering the massacre of thousands of Communists. Immediately afterward, there were divisions among the Communists, between Chen, who believed that a revolution had to be led, as in Russia, by the industrial workers, and Mao Zedong, who put his faith in the Chinese peasants. Mao in fact launched an "Autumn Harvest" peasant uprising in Hunan province in September 1927. It was premature and cruelly suppressed. Only later would Mao's views prevail.

Communist leaders Zhou Enlai, Mao and Zhu De now built up a Red Army and established a Communist state in Jiangxi province. Between 1930 and 1934 Jiang's GMD forces launched five "extermination campaigns" to destroy the Communists. Finally, in October 1934 the Red Army, facing extinction, was forced to flee to the west. One year and 9,650 kilometers (6,000 mi) later, having lost more than 90 percent of their numbers, they reached the comparative safety of Yanan. The soldiers walked over 40 kilometers (25 mi) every day. This Long March, which helped Mao Zedong gain leadership of the CCP, was one of the great feats of human endurance.

In 1931 the Japanese had taken advantage of China's civil war to seize Manchuria in

The route of the Red Army's Long March, 1934–35. Fewer than 10 percent of the original 100,000 Communists reached their destination. The march involved a battle or skirmish with hostile forces almost every day.

USSR

MANCHUKUO

Beijing

KOREA

Yanan

JAPAN

TIBET

CHINA

Chongqing

JIANGXI

FORMOSA

Mountains

Japanese land-1934

Soviets

Route of the Long March

Km 0 200 400

◄The Red Army crossing the Tatu River on May 30, 1935. It surprised GMD forces by attacking over a chain suspension bridge from which many of the planks had been removed. This feat of heroism has passed into Communist folklore.

▼Japanese troops marching through the Great Wall of China in 1933. By 1937 much of eastern China was in Japanese hands and the country suffered considerable destruction.

the northeast. In 1933 they moved farther south, to Hopei. Urged on by the Russians, in 1937 the CCP formed a second United Front with the GMD to combat the Japanese. The pact made little difference. In July 1937 the Japanese struck south, soon controlling all the more prosperous eastern half of the country. Jiang Jieshi, plentifully supplied with American arms after 1941, sat safely in his distant western stronghold of Chongqing. He was prepared to wait for the Allies to defeat Japan before relaunching his assault on the Communists.

Japan finally surrendered in 1945 after the dropping of atomic bombs on Hiroshima and Nagasaki at the end of the World War II. The stage was now set for the Red Army, aided by the large Peasant Militia, to compete with the GMD and its American ally for the control of liberated China. The victor would control the most populous nation on earth.

Mao's victory 1945-49

As the Japanese forces pulled out of China in the autumn of 1945 the Americans did what they could to prevent civil war. However, a meeting between Mao Zedong and Jiang Jieshi came to nothing, and the efforts of Generals Hurley and Marshall collapsed as fighting broke out in August 1946.

At first it looked as if Jiang's GMD was bound to win. It was supported by the Americans who gave $6 billion in aid between 1946 and 1949, and provided Jiang with 1,000 aircraft. At the Yalta Conference in 1945 the Americans had even persuaded Joseph Stalin, the Soviet leader, to back the GMD for a while. With almost four million men under his command, Jiang said that he would defeat the Communists in under a year.

The Red Army numbered fewer than a million men and had no tanks, aircraft or other heavy weapons. It was based in the countryside of northern China, the GMD having been airlifted into the northern cities by U.S. planes. However, Mao and his Generals, Lin Biao and Chen Yi, were sure they would win, but estimated that it would take up to five years.

Early in 1947 the GMD launched a massive three-pronged attack into Yanan, Shandong and Manchuria. Only in Yanan were they successful. Elsewhere, their policy of

Communist troops attacking a walled northern city in 1948 during the civil war. Because they lacked aircraft and heavy artillery, the Communists had to rely on long sieges and daring infantry attacks to seize their targets.

A rush by the citizens of Shanghai in December 1948 to get their gold out of a bank before the arrival of the People's Liberation Army. The richer classes were terrified that the Communists would seize all private wealth.

"positional warfare," concentrating their forces in important areas such as railroad junctions and towns, enabled the Communists to isolate them. In 1947 Lin Biao formed the new People's Liberation Army (PLA), and by the middle of that year Communist forces had risen to over half the numbers of the GMD. Mao left much of the fighting to his generals, concentrating instead on organizing the government and redistributing the wealth in captured areas.

Having worn down their enemy by skillful guerrilla tactics, in 1948 the PLA went on to the offensive. At the end of the year the great northern city of Mukden fell to Lin Biao, while Chen Yi took the province of Shandong. Between November 1948 and January 1949 the GMD lost half a million men in the battle of Huai-hai, opening up central China to the PLA. Beijing fell in January, and in April the PLA crossed the Chang Jiang, taking Shanghai in May. By this time Jiang, seeing his forces annihilated by the Communist tide, had fled to Formosa (now Taiwan) with his most loyal supporters. On October 1, 1949 the People's Republic of China was proclaimed. The Communists had come to power.

Weaknesses of the GMD

Mao Ke-yeh (old spelling) lived in the village of Liu Ling in northern Shaanxi province. During the civil war between the Communists and the GMD he fought as a Communist guerrilla. Later he related his experiences to the Swedish writer Jan Myrdal. Mao Ke-yeh remembered very well what the GMD soldiers were like:

> *Actually, the KMT [GMD] soldiers didn't want to fight at all. If they came to any village by themselves, we took them prisoner and gave them food and spirits and talked with them. If they wanted to go home and get out of the war, we gave them journey money and helped them to get away. In this area, around Yanan, we got about twenty KMT men a day to desert . . . People were pressed into the KMT army.*

Mao remembered, too, how unpleasant the GMD troops had been:

> *The KMT frightened people. They forced old men to carry two heavy sacks apiece, and, when they could go no farther, the KMT soldiers beat them.*

As they created such a bad impression, it is not difficult to see why Jiang Jieshi's forces found it difficult to operate successfully. Mao continued:

> *We could always move about in little groups of two or three, but there always had to be a lot of the KMT, so that they could guard each other. The officers there beat their own men, too. And the KMT also tortured its prisoners. People did not like that. So the KMT was never able to get the people on its side . . .*[1]

Jiang Jieshi and party officials lived in considerable luxury while millions of peasants starved to death. This starving refugee has been driven to gnawing at the bark of a tree in Shanghai.

Examine the picture above right of Mao Zedong and his loyal friend and adviser Zhou Enlai. They are both wearing a simple jacket to show that the Communists believed all men were equal. Jiang Jieshi, however, welcomed Western influences in China. His attitude toward the peasants was very different from Mao's. Jiang said of the peasants, "The task of the peasants is to provide us with information concerning the enemy, food, comforts and soldiers for our

armies."[2] Hearing this you can imagine how a peasant like Mao Ke-yeh might react.

There were other factors that led to the unpopularity of the GMD. Under their government there was soaring inflation. There was blatant corruption in the government and famine was widespread in GMD-controlled provinces. We saw in the last section how Jiang's unwise tactics played into the hands of the Communists. Moreover, many Chinese saw Jiang as unpatriotic because of his failure to combat the Japanese effectively, and for the way he relied on the Americans. "If Jiang supports the interests of the people," said Mao Zedong in 1946, "he is iron. If he deserts the people, and launches war against them, he is a paper tiger."[3]

▲ Mao Zedong with Zhou Enlai. Both are wearing the simple jackets, which became part of the Communist uniform.

► The GMD, led by Jiang Jieshi, relied on American support. Jiang Jieshi himself thrived on Western publicity and is here being photographed and interviewed by Western journalists.

Strengths of the Communists

The GMD was not defeated by the PLA alone, but by the people of China as a whole. In 1945 Mao Zedong had written:

> *Every comrade must be helped to understand that as long as we rely on the people, believe firmly in the inexhaustible creative power of the masses, and hence trust and identify ourselves with them, we can surmount any difficulty, and no enemy can crush us, while we can crush any enemy.*[4]

To this end Mao and his generals ensured that the Communist armies followed three basic principles: that officers and men should be treated the same, with no bullying; that civilians should always be well treated and respected; that enemy prisoners should also be well treated.

Mao Ke-yeh remembered how these principles were put into action:

> *We treated the privates well. When we captured them, they usually said: "We are farmers too. We too have parents and children and we don't like war, but want to go home to our villages." . . . we in the guerrillas never beat people and never spoke harshly to them.*

Mao also remembered how the Communists' decent behavior won friends:

> *We in the guerrillas had good sources of information. Every time the KMT asked for guides, they [the guides] got in touch with us and then we made our ambush and the KMT had a bad time of it.*[5]

Mao Zedong had commented wisely in 1946, "A people's war is not decided by taking or losing a city, but by solving the

For thousands of years the needs of the Chinese peasant class had been largely ignored by the country's rulers. These peasants lived in little more than a hole in the ground. When the Communists appeared, offering them dignity and an end to suffering, they flocked to support the new regime.

◀ Mao Zedong leading a band of peasant fighters against Jiang Jieshi in north Shaanxi in 1947. Although Mao's forces were outnumbered, Jiang Jieshi's army was suffering from corruption and a lack of morale.

▼ During the Japanese war the Red Army strengthened its hold over villages in north and central China. This peasant is teaching his son how to make a handmade grenade. The Red Army encouraged an awakening of the nationalist consciousness and established a network of political agents in the villages. This enabled it to defeat the GMD.

agrarian problem."[6] Imagine the effect on the starving families in areas "liberated" from the GMD when the Communists began to break up large estates and distribute the land among the peasants. In many areas the Communists were at work long before the PLA arrived.

In 1945 a perceptive American, who had visited the Communist-held areas of China, wrote back to Washington:

Unless the KMT goes as far as the Communists in political and economic reforms and otherwise proves itself able to contest the leadership of the people . . . the Communists will be the dominant force in China within a comparatively few years.[7]

He had summed up the situation perfectly.

Problems facing the communists

THE COMMUNIST GOVERNMENT soon discovered that the problem of governing China and introducing reforms was every bit as difficult as defeating the GMD. The country was in a terrible state. Vast tracts of arable land were under flood water, and agricultural output was at 75 percent of the 1936 level. Industrial output stood at 56 percent of the 1936 level, much machinery having been destroyed by the retreating Japanese or GMD. Only a tiny fraction of the population had any industrial skills or training, and inflation had ruined the economy.

Longer-term problems were immense. Only about 10 percent of China's 600 million people had received any education. Many Chinese were disease-ridden, undernourished and superstitious. Women were treated like animals, to be bought, sold and maltreated. Infanticide was common, as was belief in goblins, spirits and magic.

The new government, with Chairman Mao Zedong at its head, did not rush into reform. Wages and inflation were brought under control, and the currency stabilized. The need for a middle class, at least for the moment, was recognized in the Land Reform Law of 1950, which permitted the

One of the striking features of the new Communist regime was the prominent position given to Chairman Mao Zedong. This picture shows the huge portraits of Mao paraded in 1950 during the first anniversary of the Communists' rise to power.

redistribution of large estates. Only in 1954, when food shortages threatened, were peasants forced to join their private lands into cooperatives. Much industry remained in private hands, although guided by the 1953 Five Year Plan. The condition of women and children was tackled by the Marriage Law of 1950, but this met with such widespread resistance that there was a series of campaigns to raise people's consciousness on the subject. Other mass campaigns, accompanied by poster and radio propaganda, tackled a variety of problems ranging from insect pests to counterrevolutionaries.

In 1950 China made a comprehensive treaty with the USSR, its powerful Communist neighbor. Together the two countries helped the Communist regime in North Korea in its war with South Korea and the largely American-manned United Nations forces (1950–53). Otherwise China had little contact with the outside world. China

One of the main tasks of the Communist government was to reform land ownership. This propaganda poster shows a cooperative obtaining a new ox and the obvious pleasure and prosperity of everyone involved.

caused widespread protest by occupying Tibet in 1950. There were signs in 1956 that the good relations between China and the USSR were being strained.

The changes taking place in China met with considerable opposition. We do not know how many intellectuals, businessmen, landlords or conservative peasants were killed; it is estimated that between 1 and 2 million landlords died, with all other groups combined coming to fewer than that. When Mao invited criticism of his regime in 1956 with a speech famous for the phrase, "Let a hundred flowers bloom, and a hundred schools of thought contend," he was shocked at the bitterness of the response.

Land

This table explains the pattern of land ownership in the village of Longbow in 1944:

Group	Number of people	Percentage of land held
Landlord/rich peasant	63	31
Less wealthy peasant	395	45
Poor peasant	462	24
Laborer	59	0
	979	100 [8]

It is not difficult to see that well over half the people in the village had to live off less than a quarter of the land. The result of such a pattern of land-holding was a large increase in the number of starving peasants.

But the problem for the Communists was not just eliminating starvation. In their land reforms they had two other aims. They hoped to tax increased agricultural production to obtain money to invest in China's backward industry. Second, they wanted to tie the peasants to the new regime and eliminate those who might lead a counterrevolution.

Land was redistributed by the Land Reform Law of June 28, 1950. The peasants were divided into three groups: rich (those who received more than 25 percent of their income from the labor of others), averagely well off, and poor. Three hundred million peasants were given a total of over 700 million *mous* of land (one *mou* is about one acre). The minimum a peasant could be given was 2–3 *mous*, so the average family received about 2.5 acres.

This 1951 propaganda poster is entitled "Ready to submit a production report to Mao Zedong." These men and women are working together on a cooperative. The amount and variety of goods shown suggests that life for the peasant has improved.

An example of a "people's court." The whole village crowds around as judges hear the case.

Many of the new farms were too small to be economically viable. At first the farmers were encouraged to form Mutual Aid Teams, whereby they helped each other with the harvest; then cooperatives were formed in which they shared equipment and animals. Finally by 1957 about 97 percent of all peasants had been joined into collectives, where all land – except for small plots of about 60 square meters (645 sq ft) per family – machinery and animals were held in common.

When land was taken from the landlords in 1950 there was much cruelty and suffering, particularly at the hands of village courts similar to the one shown above. Here is a description, based upon what really happened, of how one landlord named Chien was treated:

One accusation was brought after another . . . Some peasants were so carried away that they climbed onto the stage and struck at Chien as they questioned him, while the crowd backed them up: "Beat him, beat him to death!" [9]

We do not know how many millions of people died in the Land Reform. Later, most peasants seem to have joined cooperatives quite willingly, but there was some resistance. For example, almost 20 percent of the pigs in China were killed by their owners rather than handed over to communes. Agricultural production during the first Five Year Plan rose 4.5 percent a year, but since the population was rising at 2.3 percent a year, this increase in agricultural production was not sufficient to subsidize industrial advance.

Society, women and culture

The aim of the Communists was nothing less than the total transformation of Chinese society. One of their most striking reforms was the Marriage Law of May 1, 1950:

Article 1
The arbitrary and compulsory feudal marriage system, which is based on the superiority of man over women and which ignores the children's interests, shall be abolished.

The New Democratic marriage system, which is based upon free choice of partners, on monogamy, on equal rights for both sexes, and on protection of the lawful interests of women and children, shall be put into effect.

Article 2
Bigamy, concubinage, child betrothal, interference with the remarriage of widows, and the exaction of money or gifts in connection with marriage shall be prohibited.

Article 4
A marriage can be contracted only after a man has reached 20 years of age and a woman has reached 18 years of age.

Article 13
. . . Infanticide by drowning and similar criminal acts are strictly prohibited.[10]

But there was a considerable difference between issuing a law in Beijing and seeing that it was carried out in the provinces. As late as 1982 Jonathan Mirsky wrote in the British newspaper *The Observer*:

> *Chinese peasants are allowing their baby girls to die at such a rate that a call has gone out to save them. Nothing but murder or deliberate neglect can explain why in some communes just 200 girls survive out of every 500 children born.*[11]

Even Chairman Mao did not set a good example of treatment of women. When still married to Yang Kaihui, he met and lived with He Zizhen. After Yang's death he married He, and she accompanied him on the Long March. But when He went to Russia in 1937 to have her war wounds treated, Mao fell in love with the beautiful actress Jiang Qing. Mao divorced He, married

This typical propaganda picture is entitled "After a rich harvest." Plentiful crops and a high standard of living was promised to those who toed the party line and worked hard.

Jiang and later used the power of state censorship to remove all traces of his action.

Although the Chinese people benefited enormously from improved education, medical services, housing, food and social legislation, the country was never free. It was impossible to be successful without being a member of the Communist Party, and there were frequent purges of potential antirevolutionary groups. But tight government control was necessary to achieve rapid economic growth.

◄ Tibetan women being taught to read. Between 1950 and 1960 the number of teachers in China rose from ½ million to 2½ million, and the number of elementary school pupils doubled to 100 million.

▼ A poster showing the registration of a marriage that has been decided on by free choice rather than having been arranged.

Industry

The Australian historian, Bruce McFarlane, wrote of China's economic development in the 1950s:

> *At the time of the revolution in 1949 the Chinese economy was a shambles, with industrial and agricultural output well below their previous peak levels. China was one of the poorest countries in the world. Yet, by 1960, China had shown the world a rate of economic growth greater than that achieved by most other countries. The gross national product between 1950 and 1959 grew by more than 10 percent per annum in real terms (that is allowing for price rises). These substantial gains were based on a heavy investment program in machinery, averaging about 25 percent of total output . . . One result was that industrial production rose during the decade at an average annual rate of 20 percent.*[12]

This table shows industrial output of various commodities up to 1957:

Item	1949	1957
Steel prod.	158,000 tons	5.4 million tons
Coal prod.	32 million tons	130 million tons
Electricity prod.	4,310 kWh	19,000, kWh
Rail tracks built	21,715 km (13,463 mi)	44,000 km (27,000 mi)
Roads built	80,000 km (49,600 mi)	400,000 km (248,000 mi)
Tractor prod.	0	8,500 [13]

As the table indicates, the major achievement during the first eight years of Communist rule was the dramatic increase in industrial output.

The development of roads and railroads helped to open up some of the inaccessible western areas of China.

The Communists did not seize all private industry when they came to power, but they gradually taxed firms and individuals more and more heavily. In the end, owners found it easier to hand over their plants to the state

One of the first tasks of the new government in 1949 was to get the nation's communications running properly. This railroad track is being built to connect mines with an iron and steel works.

▲ One of the consequences of the 1950 Marriage Law was that women were treated as equal to men in all things. Here they are seen hauling stones in a major construction project.

and run them as managers or advisers.

Han Suyin was born in China but was abroad when the Communists seized power in 1949. In 1956 she returned to meet her family and recalled her engineer father's reminiscences of the early years of Communist rule:

> *The railroads started running, and a new railroad was built within two years, 1950–52, between Chengdu and Chongqing, in Sichuan. "It's the railroad that I came back to build in 1913," Papa reminisced, laughing and creasing his eyes. In 1952, when the first locomotive, beflagged and all its loudspeakers singing, had rolled into the new station in Chengdu, where crowds danced and beat drums, an old engineer, overcome with emotion, had knelt and kissed the steel rails. He too had wanted, all his life, to build a railroad for his country.*[14]

Workers tending their rice crop. The government relied heavily upon the surplus made on the farms to finance industrial advance, although workers were not always willing to see their profits creamed off for other projects.

Foreign relations

Since the Opium Wars of the early nineteenth century, China had been bullied by other nations. The Russians, Japanese, British, Germans, French and others had all either helped themselves directly to pieces of Chinese territory or else had established their own "spheres of influence." From being the most powerful and civilized state on earth, as it had been in earlier times, China had become a third-rate power, plundered and manipulated by anyone with up-to-date armed forces. In the light of this, examine the statement of Mao Zedong

Mao Zedong signing an agreement with the USSR in 1957. Even by this date there were signs of growing tension between the two nations.

on October 1, 1949, announcing the new republic:

> *We proclaim the setting up of the People's Republic of China. Henceforth, our nation will from now on enter the large family of peace-loving and freedom-loving nations of the world. It will work bravely to create its own civilization and happiness and will at the same time promote world peace and freedom. Our nation will never again be an insulted nation. We have stood up. Our revolution has gained the sympathy and acclamation of the broad masses throughout the world. We have friends the world over.*[15]

It may be worth considering what Mao meant by "freedom-loving." He was probably referring to his people's freedom from foreign oppression, rather than the more Western idea of freedom for individuals to do as they wished politically. It is also interesting to see how Mao interpreted his idea of promoting world peace.

China may have had friends all over the world, but few of them were in positions of influence. The only great power to show true friendship was the USSR. In February 1950 the two countries signed a treaty of Friendship, Alliance and Mutual Assistance, which was said to be "everlasting and unbreakable." Thousands of Soviet scientists and technicians came to help the Chinese develop their economy. By 1959 the USSR had helped China with 336 major projects and given the country millions of rubles worth of aid. Chinese Communism, with its economic development, the Five Year Plan and control by the party, mirrored that of the USSR. When in 1950 United Nations troops, led by the United States, invaded North Korea on China's border, Soviet aid and Chinese troops poured in successfully to resist the invaders.

But inspite of Mao's claims that China has "stood up," the country was now dependent on the USSR. China was cut off economically from the dominant West and prevented by the United States from joining the United Nations.

A map showing China and neighboring countries in 1950.

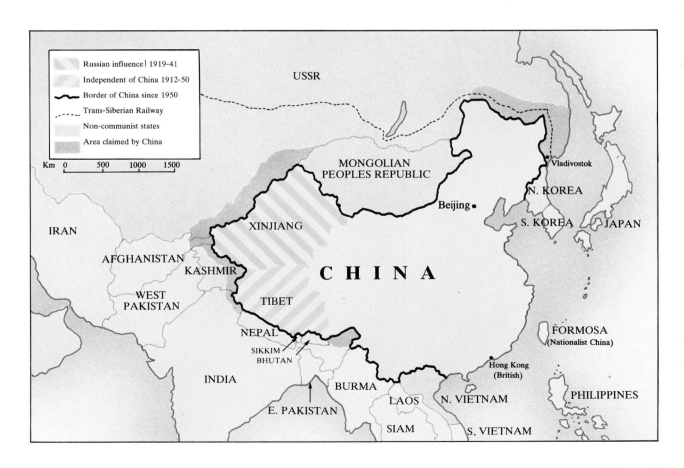

Left and right turns 1957–66

THE FIRST EIGHT YEARS of Communist rule in China had gone well. Industry and agriculture had flourished and the new government was widely accepted throughout the country. Abroad, friendship with the USSR had brought many benefits, while the might of the United States had been checked in Korea. In comparison, the years from 1957 to 1966 were full of turmoil.

No one really knows why Mao Zedong made his famous "One Hundred Flowers" speech in 1956, but we do know that he did not like the result; all over China posters, articles and meetings criticized the government. Mao admitted that 30 percent of the population supported the Communists, 30 percent were hostile, and the others remained indifferent. His response to this was in 1957 to end the Hundred Flowers period, deal with the opposition, and in 1958 call for a Great Leap Forward.

The Great Leap Forward was something entirely new. It aimed to do two things: dramatically increase industrial and agricultural production and develop Communist attitudes among the people. Mao felt that the momentum of the revolution was slowing. He was also coming under personal criticism: in 1959 he resigned as Chairman of the People's Republic of China, although

▶ A block of apartments in Machaio commune near Shanghai. In some communes workers were not permitted to keep even their own pots and pans or bicycles. Their houses were knocked down to make way for large dormitory buildings.

◀ Members of a commune in central China threshing grain. There were originally 26,000 communes in China. After their failure to produce agricultural and industrial goods efficiently by 1962 they were broken up into smaller units about one-third of their original size.

he remained party Chairman; and after an internal squabble he broke with his old friend and fellow soldier Peng Dehuai.

To bring about the Great Leap Forward, in 1958 the rural population of China was organized into huge communes, each containing about 40,000 people. In these 26,000 self-sufficient units, most goods were held in common – in some, families were broken up as men and women slept together in large dormitories. Economic progress was to be brought about by mass peasant labor, not by large-scale sophisticated industrial processes.

All this was very different from the pattern of Communism in the USSR. In fact, since 1958 relations between China and the USSR had become very strained. Nikita Khrushchev, the new Soviet leader, scorned the cult of Mao and his communes. In 1960 Soviet engineers and scientists were recalled to the USSR and Soviet aid dried up. This coincided with three years of terrible natural disasters, flood and drought (1959–61) in which as many as 20 million Chinese died. Conflict with India (1961–62), along the southern borders of China only made matters worse.

By 1960 the Great Leap Forward was no longer mentioned. It had failed. The communes were subdivided, some private enterprise was encouraged again, and the economy began to pick up. But the damage had been extensive.

The communist path in China

Lin Biao inspecting the Red Army in 1959. Lin was one of Mao's staunchest allies during the difficult late 1950s. He became Minister of Defense in 1959, in place of Peng Dehuai, and he made sure that the army was always loyal to Mao.

Modern Communism has its origins in the Western industrialized nations of the nineteenth century, with large urban working classes. It was felt that society had to pass from a feudal state through an industrial, capitalist phase before there could be a true communist, or socialist, revolution. Marx, for example, had said that he did not believe socialist revolution likely in Russia for a long time because Russia had no large urban working class.

One of the great contributions of Lenin to the theories of communism was the idea that the socialist revolution should be led by a group of dedicated, professional revolutionaries. Using the small but politically minded Russian industrial working class, he successfully engineered the Russian revolution in 1917. Under Lenin and then under Stalin, the USSR set about building up its industrial, scientific and technological strength, at the same time attempting to develop its agriculture. This was done through strict state control, terrorization of the peasantry and a series of Five Year Plans.

As we have seen, China gratefully followed the USSR's pattern of development in the early 1950s, except in its treatment of the peasantry. When Stalin died in 1953, Mao said of him:

> Everyone knows that Comrade Stalin had a great love for the Chinese people and believed in the mighty Chinese Revolution. He gave his great wisdom to helping with the problems of revolution. It was by following the theories of Lenin and Stalin and with the support of the great Soviet Union that the Chinese Communist Party and the Chinese people a few years ago won their historic victory.[16]

Mao seemed to be choosing to forget that in 1945 Stalin had favored Jiang Jieshi and in 1927, after Jiang's butchering of the Communists, he had continued for a while to back the GMD.

Mao hated the United States, the power that had invaded Korea and supported Jiang Jieshi: "Riding roughshod everywhere, U.S. imperialism has made itself the enemy of the people of the world."[17] The Americans were, he claimed, "paper tigers." Imagine Mao's reaction when Khrushchev visited the United States in 1959, seeking friendlier relations between the USSR and the United States: "Anyone who thinks that Communism can be advanced by war," said Khrushchev, "belongs to the lunatic asylum." Mao's view was radically different:

We may lose more than 300 million people. So what? War is war. Time will pass and we'll start producing more babies.[18]

So Mao turned from the Soviets and the intellectuals, to those who had first brought him to power:

The masses have boundless creative power. They can organize themselves and concentrate on places and branches of work where they can give full play to their energy.[19]

They were to be the driving force in the Great Leap Forward.

This poster published in Canton after the Great Leap Forward shows Red Guards crushing the figure representing imperialism, in defense of the revolution.

Communes

In 1955 Mao Zedong wrote:

> *There is a serious tendency toward capitalism among the well-to-do peasants. This tendency will become rampant if we in the slightest way neglect political work among the peasants during the cooperative movement and for a very long period after.*[20]

Jan Myrdal found a good example of Mao's "serious tendency toward capitalism" when he talked to Li Hai-guan, the labor leader of a cooperative. Li, despite the protests of his fellow workers, decided to leave his cooperative and set up on his own:

> *I didn't care what they said; the main thing was for me to get those two oxen, and be on my own. In the end, the others had to agree to it, of course . . . I worked harder than ever before.*[21]

But the Communist leaders could not allow this sort of behavior to continue.

The picture below shows workers on a commune operating a treadmill to force water through the irrigation ditches of a paddy field. Although this method of irrigation was not very efficient, for the Communist leaders it had important political effects on the workers themselves. No one could operate the system on their own; cooperation was essential.

But the effects of the move to communes were not just political, as this table shows:

Item	1957	1960	
Grain production	295.05 million tons	143.5 million tons	
Grain ration per person for the year	203 kilos (447 lb)	163.5 kilos (360 lb)	[22]

A team of four men operating a treadmill.

The crisis in Chinese agriculture was so severe that many town-dwellers were called upon to help farm the land. Here soldiers are helping farmers carry fertile soil to the fields.

The figures reveal that the output of grain actually fell sharply during these years. However, these figures are distorted by the fact that there was a series of natural disasters in China at this time, which only made matters worse. Whatever system of production was used, levels of production might well have fallen.

Peng Dehuai was Minister of Defense until 1959. He was critical of the communes, as this passage explains:

Peng came upon a large pile of ripe crops lying on the ground apparently abandoned. After a lengthy search, an old peasant was finally located who explained that all the able-bodied people were busy launching a steel sputnik [i.e. attempting to set a record in steel production]. Peng exclaimed: "Hasn't any one of you given a thought to what you will eat next year if you don't bring in the crops? You're never going to be able to eat steel." The old peasant nodded vigorously in agreement, but added pointedly, "True enough. Who would disagree with that? But who can stand up against the wind?"[23]

Was the "wind" of the Great Leap Forward really necessary?

Industry

The photograph below captures exactly the spirit of the Great Leap Forward. It shows an army of workers building a canal. Their enthusiasm is matched by that of Mao's poem of 1963 entitled, "Seize the Day, Seize the Hour!":

On this tiny globe
A few flies dash themselves against the wall,
Humming without cease,
Sometimes shrilling,
Sometimes moaning.
Ants on the locust tree assume a great
   nation swagger
And mayflies lightly plot to topple the giant tree.
The west wind scatters leaves over Changan,
And the arrows are flying, twanging.

So many deeds cry out to be done,
And always urgently;
The world rolls on,
Time presses.
Ten thousand years are too long,
Seize the day, seize the hour!

The Four Seas are rising, clouds and waters
   raging.
The Five Continents are rocking, wind and
   thunder roaring.
Away with all pests:
Our force is irresistible.[24]

Despite the urgency of Mao's poem (Khrushchev was probably one of his "few flies") and the energetic chaos of the canal building scene below, mistakes were made during the Great Leap: measurements were inaccurate, safety standards were ignored, planning was inadequate and much energy was wasted.

One of the most unusual aspects of the Great Leap Forward's industrial program

During the Great Leap Forward large-scale projects were set up to improve industry. In building this canal it was intended that the right political spirit and sheer force of numbers would overcome the problem of the lack of machinery.

An important steel mill, which grew during the Great Leap Forward.

was the setting up of thousands of backyard steel plants. But, here again the Chinese faced the same problems, as this Soviet observer (somewhat exaggeratedly) noted:

According to the official figure, 4 million tons of iron were processed, but of this amount hardly more than 1 percent was usable, the remaining 99 percent being slag, unwashed ore, or even more often, a pure invention of the statistician. [25]

Examine the figures for production during the second part of the Great Leap Forward. They tell us the story of the effect of the Great Leap Forward on the Chinese economy.

89-17046

Item	1959	1962
Coal production	347.80	270.00
Steel production	13.30	7.10
Crude oil	3.70	5.60

(All figures in million tons) [26]

Over the same period Chinese exports fell by $500 million.

Mao later admitted, "I understand nothing about industrial planning . . . we rushed into a great catastrophe . . . You [referring to himself] must be more cautious." [27]

Mao's later years 1966–76

DURING THE EARLY 1960S Mao felt power slipping from his hands. He was now getting old and he had been blamed for the failures of the Great Leap Forward. Control in China passed to Liu Shaoqi, the head of state, and Deng Xiaoping, general secretary of the central committee. Under the new leadership, private enterprise was once more permitted, private plots of land were allowed, family life was restored and economic incentives for hard work were introduced. Mao felt that the revolution was losing its way, as personal gain and greed replaced service to the state.

In 1966 Mao made his move. He swam 15 kilometers (9 mi) down the Chang Jiang River to show that he was in excellent health, then he closed all secondary schools and universities, and summoned the students to Beijing. In a series of rallies he told them that the revolution was in danger. They, as Red Guards, had to save it. "Smash the old and bring in the new!" he urged.

For two years there followed total chaos in China. Gangs of youths, in a "uniform" of dull green jackets, baggy trousers that were modeled on the army uniform, and red armbands, went about bullying, arresting or killing anyone in any way suspected of counterrevolutionary ideas. Even owning a necktie was sufficient excuse for a beating. Liu died in prison, Deng disappeared for a while. Books were burned, records smashed. The only acceptable guideline was *The Little Red Book of Collected Thoughts of Chairman Mao*. Indeed, Mao was seen almost as a god: "Father is dear, Mother is dear," chanted the Red Guards, "but Chairman Mao is dearest of all."

By 1968 the country was verging on civil war as groups of Red Guards clashed with each other and with their opponents. So Mao used the army to break up the most unruly groups of Red Guards, and he ordered several million young people from the cities into the countryside, to learn from the peasants. Law and order gradually

School children marching during the Cultural Revolution. No one, not even leading politicians, was safe from interrogation by the Red Guards.

returned, but the Cultural Revolution did not officially end until Mao's death in 1976. Censorship remained strict, art dull and private profit forbidden. But Mao was in charge once more.

One dramatic development of the early 1970s was the reestablishment of friendly relations between China and the United States. In 1969, after Soviet and Chinese troops had clashed on the Ussuri River, China felt the need to end its isolation. In 1971 the U.S. Secretary of State, Henry Kissinger, visited China, followed the next year by President Nixon. China was admitted to membership in the United Nations in 1971 and Taiwan had to leave: after twenty-two years in the wilderness, China had finally come in from the cold.

► A meeting of factory workers in 1967 in which they are repudiating the influence of capitalists in the party and in the factory. They also take time to study the thoughts of Chairman Mao.

► A poster published in 1966 entitled "Mao Zedong is the red sun of our hearts." In it young people representing different ethnic minorities within China are rallying to defend Mao and the revolution.

毛主席是我们心中的红太阳

The lost generation

Here is an excerpt from the Declaration of Red Guards on February 22, 1967:

> *Since their birth, the Red Guards have been active on the historic stage of the proletarian revolution as a political shock force, showing a dauntless, revolutionary rebel spirit . . . The Red Guards, taking the invincible thought of Mao Tse-tung as their weapon and having the powerful support of the workers, peasants and soldiers, have swept aside ghosts and monsters . . . energetically destroyed the old ideas, culture, customs, and habits of the exploiting classes and vigorously fostered the new ideas, culture, customs.*[28]

Most young people want to rebel, to challenge the values and customs of the older generation. Much of what they have to say is valuable. However, they may also be prone to violence. Mao thought that he was correct in using the natural rebelliousness of the young "to stimulate the masses to dismantle the anti-Mao bureaucracy."[29]

This is the sort of thing that went on:

> *A girl remembered a really freezing day when she and her friends made three of the teachers from their school kneel on the ground outside without their coats or gloves. After that the leader of their group . . . told them to beat the teachers. They found some wooden boards and the pupils started hitting the teachers. "We kept on till one of the teachers started coughing up blood . . . We felt very proud of ourselves. It seemed very revolutionary."*[30]

> *. . . sometimes a person with a grudge invents a story. Our daughter had bought a bag in Shanghai. It was prettier than the Peking ones, and a neighbor coveted it. She told the Red Guards that we had foreign goods, and they turned up everything in our house, dug up the floors and the garden, chipped plaster off the walls to uncover gold pieces or documents. They took away books, pictures, vases, anything . . .*[31]

It is interesting to compare the pictures on these pages of the masses adoring Mao with this statement by an ex-Red Guard:

> *Chairman Mao said we were supposed to learn from the peasants, but the peasants didn't want anything to do with us . . . They thought we were lazy. They blamed us for eating all their food without earning it.*[32]

◄ Children gathering around Chairman Mao. During the Cultural Revolution Mao was seen almost as a god; factory meetings ended with the chant "May the Chairman live ten thousand years."

以毛泽东思想为武器

横扫一切牛鬼蛇神

彻底揭露
彻底批判
彻底打倒

◄ A propaganda poster published in July 1966. Young people rally to support the Cultural Revolution. A man holds a poster bearing an extract from the works of Chairman Mao.

Most schools and universities closed during the Cultural Revolution, with the result that of the 140 million Chinese who were illiterate in 1981, 120 million were under 45 years old.

One girl commented in 1980 that "Her eyes were opened by the Cultural Revolution. She saw through the Communists."[33] Had Mao in fact saved the revolution or destroyed it?

► A demonstration in which each man is holding his copy of *The Little Red Book of the Collected Thoughts of Chairman Mao.* These thoughts were held to be so brilliant that, if applied correctly, they could do anything, from improving factory production to replacing formal education.

The economy

When Han Suyin was in China during the Cultural Revolution she remembered how the *Thoughts of Chairman Mao* were said to hold the key to economic advance:

> *. . . production has gone up by so much . . . everywhere, owing to the "heightening of revolutionary consciousness" among the workers. Production increase is no longer ascribed to the heroic, the fantastic, the real work of the marvelous, incredibly patient and stoic people of China, but solely to the study of Mao Tse-tung Thought.*[34]

This quotation is from Han Suyin's book published in 1980. During the Cultural Revolution, however, she had nothing but praise for all that it stood for. Yet the most practical advice in Mao's Thoughts is "Natural science is one of man's weapons in his fight for freedom . . . man must use natural science to understand, conquer and change nature and thus attain freedom from nature."[35]

Sometimes blind adherence to Mao's thoughts could do positive harm. Han Suyin recalls an example of this. In 1964 Mao praised the commune of Dazhai in the hilly Shaanxi province as a model for all others.

The fields of Dazhai were terraces cut into the hillsides. A commune that Han Suyin saw in Manchuria was on a flat plain, but the workers had piled up vast heaps of earth into man-made hills, into which to cut terraces:

> *The mounds that I saw were all artificial; they had been raised up and fields laddered upon them to resemble Dazhai. That is how "In all things learn from Dazhai" [Mao's words] had been interpreted by the literal-minded Cadres.*[36]

During 1967–68 the Cultural Revolution, with its slogan of "Politics takes command of the economy and revolution comes before production," upset the Chinese economy. But this slogan did not last long. From about early 1969 onward, the slogan was "Promote Revolution, Grasp Production"; namely revolution and food were considered equally important.

Students at work on an agricultural commune. Some argued that the Cultural Revolution helped to break down the barriers between the different groups in Chinese society, thus making the country more cohesive and productive.

The chart below shows China's industrial output during the Cultural Revolution.

Workers in a chemical fertilizer plant studying a production graph in 1966. They have fulfilled their target.

	Cultural Revolution					
	1966	1967	1968	1969	1970	1974
Grain output	190	190	180	210	—	270
Coal production	230	190	190	210	300	400
Oil production	12	12	12	—	20	26
Steel production	12	10	8	9	13	25
Chemical fertilizer	9	7	8	9	14	25
(All figures in millions of tons)						
Overall industrial output as a percentage of 1966	—	80%	70%	90%	100%	200%
Value of China's foreign trade in millions of dollars	4,391	3,807	3,620	3,873	4,246	12,000 [37]

The Cultural Revolution had a damaging effect on the Chinese economy up to 1969. But once the country had gone back to work, it is interesting to see how quickly the effects of the Cultural Revolution on the economy were overcome. Indeed, some historians have seen the overall effects of the Cultural Revolution as being beneficial to Chinese industry:

The increase in industrial production between 1964 and 1974 was due to new relations established in factories: workers, cadres, and technicians . . . worked together in devising new projects, machines and products, and in improving the quality and quantity of production.[38]

Foreign relations

One of the most remarkable changes in Chinese policy between 1956 and 1976 was the reversal in its policy of friendship with the USSR and hostility to the United States. On December 10, 1970, Edgar Snow, an American journalist, spoke at some length with Mao Zedong. Their conversation showed how the Chairman's views had altered from the days when he wrote of the United States as "the most murderous of hangmen" and his friendship with the USSR as "perfectly true and sincere."[39]

"Do the Russians fear China?" Snow asked:

It was said that they were a bit afraid, he [Mao] answered. Even when there are a few mice in a person's room the person could become frightened, fearful that the mice might eat up his sweets . . .

The Russians looked down on the Chinese and also looked down on the people of many countries, he said. They thought that they had only to speak the word and all people would listen and obey. They did not believe that there were people who would not do so and that one of them was his humble self.

► President Nixon and Mao Zedong in their historic meeting in Beijing in February 1972. For Mao, friendship with the United States was a complete reversal of China's previous policy, but it was in the best interests of China, which felt threatened by the USSR on its northern border.

◄ Chinese tanks on the frontier with Vietnam in 1978. The Chinese gave considerable aid to the North Vietnamese in their struggle with South Vietnam and the United States, but after the American withdrawal (1973) and the defeat of the South (1975) the country has come under more Soviet influence.

Mao also spoke of Sino-American relations:

. . . between Chinese and Americans there need be no prejudices. There could be mutual respect and equality. He said he placed high hopes on the peoples of the two countries.

Mao concluded:

. . . that China should learn from the way America developed, by decentralizing and spreading responsibility and wealth among the fifty states.[40]

Once relations between the USSR and China had soured, Mao's main fear was of the USSR. By 1970 U.S. troops were pulling out of Vietnam, leaving the country under Soviet influence. In fact there was fighting between China and Vietnam in 1979. Kampuchea and Laos came under Vietnamese influence. The USSR had massive forces along its 7,241-km (4,500-mi) border with China; there had been armed clashes at several points, notably on the Ussuri River in 1969.

The United States and the USSR were hostile to each other, so an approach to the United States in the early 1970s made practical sense for China. In spite of the fact that the USSR was a fellow Communist state, Mao, when faced with the political realities of the situation, pursued a policy of friendship toward the United States.

Modernization of the revolution

BY THE EARLY 1970S it was clear that Mao Zedong was once more losing his grip on affairs in China. Two factions had emerged, contesting for control of the country when the great leader would die. On one hand was Deng Xiaoping, the veteran politician who wanted to see his country advance along a moderate road, mixing the best of China's Communism with the most advantageous aspects of Western capitalism. To some extent he was supported by Zhou Enlai, Mao's most likely successor. In 1975 Zhou announced his "Four Modernizations" campaign to update agriculture, industry, science and technology, and the armed forces. This involved proposals for considerable relaxation of state control.

Deng was opposed by a group of more extremist politicians, known as the Gang of Four. They were Jiang Qing, (Mao's wife), Wang Hongwen, Zhang Chunqiao and Yao Wenyuan. Their aim was to maintain the strict policies of the Cultural Revolution. By and large, they could count on Mao Zedong's support.

Some months after Zhou died in January 1976, there were huge demonstrations of loyalty to him. These were in fact popular protests against the Gang of Four and their drab policies of repression and state control. Deng was blamed for the riots and removed

Mao's successor, Hua Guofeng. Shortly after coming to power in 1976, Hua surprised many by arresting the group of Maoists known as the Gang of Four. Within a couple of years, however, Hua himself was overshadowed by the pragmatic Deng Xiaoping.

A street demonstration in October 1976 against the Gang of Four and in support of Hua Guofeng. The poster shows the Gang of Four with a bayonet struck through them. It demonstates the strength of feeling against the Gang of Four.

from office. He was replaced as Vice-Chairman by Hua Guofeng, whom Mao had chosen to succeed him. But barely a month after Mao's death in September, Hua arrested the Gang of Four, bringing Deng back to office in the following year.

Since 1977 Deng Xiaoping has been the most influential man in China, Hua being officially demoted in 1981. Although the Cultural Revolution was declared closed in 1977, the Mao line is still strongly supported in the CCP, and Deng has had to tread carefully so as not to annoy conservatives such as Chen Yun.

The main features of Deng's government have been:

1 Closer cooperation with the West, for example signing commercial treaties with Japan (1978) and the United States (1979);
2 A very strict "one child per family" birth control program (1980);
3 Economic modernization along the lines called for in the "Four Modernizations."

This has involved the abolition of the communes and a return to household-based farming, the introduction of some private enterprise, and working more closely with the West;
4 Attempts at political reform. Those in favor of greater democracy call this the "fifth modernization." There were strong popular protests in its support in 1978–79 and 1986–87. But Deng had to abandon his plans for political reforms in 1980 in the face of conservative opposition; and the protests of 1986–87 led to the dismissal of Deng's right-hand man, Hu Yaobang. China, it seems, is still far from being a politically stable country.

Failure of the Gang of Four

The Gang of Four and their supporters, who upheld the rigid revolutionary Communism of the Cultural Revolution, were arrested in 1976 and put on trial in 1981.

Perhaps half a million people died as a result of the Cultural Revolution. Millions more suffered educational, cultural and economic deprivation. Lihua, who spoke to the American reporter Fox Butterfield, recalled what the Revolution meant to her:

> *I want people outside China to know what the Cultural Revolution was like and what the Chinese people have been through . . . I've never lived a good day in my life. My mother was beaten to death, my father was left senseless. That is what the Cultural Revolution did . . . My scars will never heal.*[41]

By 1974, according to Han Suyin who had spent some time in the West, there was great fear in China that the ways of the Cultural Revolution might return. She was in the country then and reported:

> *A miasma [nasty fog] of disquiet in the air. It is due to the Dragon Lady, Chiang Ching . . . My insistence that she is irresponsible, mentally deranged, is unacceptable to my friends. They see in her a willful demoniac [devil], and the muttering of dislike of 1972 is changing into an almost pathological hatred. Everything that went wrong, every cruelty, every death, is now her fault. "There isn't a family in China which has not suffered because of her," said Hualan.*

Han Suyin continues to record the strong hostility she noticed toward the Gang of Four. They were blamed for causing steel workers to strike, for encouraging male prostitution and immorality, for encouraging the young once more to become "insolent, rude and lazy." Jiang Qing was accused of importing Western films (not permitted in China) for her own viewing; she was known in secret as the Devil, the Plague or the Witch. Mao himself is even reported as having said to his wife, "You are far too ambitious. You four . . . you stick together, forming a gang, like in the bad old days of the Mafia in Shanghai. Do not form a gang of four . . . no good will come of it."

According to Han Suyin, for a time after Mao's death it looked as if another Cultural Revolution would begin:

Jiang Qing, Mao's detested widow, at her trial. She defended herself against the charge leveled at her by saying, "I was Mao's dog. Whoever he told me to bite, I bit!"

A scientist was . . . attacked. "When the earth satellite went up in the sky, the red flag came down to earth . . . Down with science, which destroys revolution!" shouted the young who assaulted him. His laboratory instruments were smashed.

Then came the news of Hua's action in arresting the Gang of Four. "I could not believe it," wrote Han Suyin:

It seemed too good to be true. All my friends in China had the same reaction . . . China was exuberant. There were monstrous parades, millions pouring into the streets to celebrate, to beat drums and dance.[42]

As Mao had captured the mood of the people in 1947–49, so, perhaps, had Hua Guofeng in 1976.

Deng's China

Deng Xiaoping's aims are these:

1 To stimulate the economy by
   - allowing individuals to make private profit by selling surplus production, particularly in agriculture;
   - encouraging foreign firms to go into partnerships with Chinese concerns;
   - borrowing foreign capital;
   - disbanding communes and cooperatives and allowing private farms;
   - permitting manufacturers to react more to market forces;
   - cutting the birth rate.
2 To modernize China's armed forces by using foreign equipment.
3 To bring China up-to-date in the fields of science and technology, by investing in their development, and giving educational and other advantages to more able students.

4 To make China a more open society through –
   - decentralization;
   - separating the CCP from economic and governmental activities;
   - extending civil rights and building a functioning legal system.

The political and economic problems connected with Deng's policies are examined in the next section. For the moment let us concentrate on one of the single most controversial decisions of his premiership, the One-Child Policy of 1980.

The booming city of Tianjin in northern China in 1986. The huge new hotel in the center of the picture was built with the help of money and expertise from Hong Kong.

Examine these statements:

- In the last thirty years the population of China has doubled, from about 500 million to over 1 billion.
- If Chinese families average three children each, the population of the country will be 2 billion by the year 2035, and 3 billion by 2075.
- In 1900 the average length of life in China was about 27 years. It is now over 70.
- More than two-thirds of the Chinese are under 24 years of age.
- In the early 1980s China was spending millions of U.S. dollars importing grain to feed its population.

When faced with figures like this, the task of China's leaders was clear: cut the birth rate and increase food production. But how? It was not realistic to expect couples to have no children, so the minimum reasonable number was one child per family. If each couple has one child the population will still

Rewards are given to those who have limited their families to one child. These women are being given financial rewards. All mothers who have a single baby receive a 5 percent bonus on their earnings, free medical care for the child and extra food.

rise to 1.2 billion, before falling back to 600 million in a hundred years time.

Today, in order to get married, couples have to be over 24 years old and pass an exam in family planning. They then have to obtain permission from their Brigade Family Planning Officer to have their one child. Contraceptives are free, and couples who have more than one child suffer serious economic penalties.

Perhaps this is an unacceptable restriction on personal freedom. Certainly it has led to thousands of babies, especially girls, being killed. Girls are killed because of a desire to continue the family name (via the male line) and because of a traditional contempt for women.

Forward or backward?

A discarded picture of Chairman Mao. Under Deng Xiaoping the cult of Mao has waned, and some criticism of his excesses, particularly during the Cultural Revolution, have been voiced.

China must with energy follow the Four Modernizations of farming, industry, defense and science. This does not mean shutting the door on the world or blindly opposing all that is foreign.[43]

The tensions that have occurred in China since Deng Xiaoping came to power boil down to two questions. Is China betraying the Communist revolution if it introduces principles and practices from the West that help its economy? Second, how far dare the authorities increase personal freedom?

Deng argued at the Chinese Science Conference in 1978:

His line is supported by a wall poster that appeared in 1978: "The Cultural Revolution must be reassessed. Mao Zedong was 70 percent good and 30 percent bad."

At his trial in 1979 the liberal reformer Wei Jingsheng argued:

I must point out that freedom of speech is not a wild allegation but is stipulated in black and white in the Constitution. It is a right which every citizen should enjoy.[44]

Critics of Deng called his reforms mere "bourgeois liberalism," although Deng himself was the most vocal opponent of "bourgeois liberalism." One paper stated:

It is necessary to import advanced foreign technology, but we must essentially rely on our own strength . . . As a socialist country we should keep an independent economic system and follow our own path for developing industry . . . The technical projects of the capitalist countries are based on the search for super profits by the capitalist monopolists: thus they bear the incontestable stigma of class.[45]

The conservatives point to the fact that since market forces have been allowed to play a part in China's economy, unemployment has soared. Why has this happened?

The last word rests with the Prosecutor of Wei Jingsheng at his trial:

Our Constitution clearly stipulates extensive democratic rights. However, our democracy should be a democracy protected by law. It does not mean absolute freedom for one to do as one likes . . . Freedom of speech of the individual citizen must be based upon the four basic principles of insisting on the socialist road, the dictatorship of the proletariat, the leadership of the party, and Marxist-Leninism – Mao Zedong Thought. The citizen has only the freedom to support these principles and not the freedom to oppose them . . .

If . . . individualistic freedom of the minority is allowed to run rampant, the freedom of the majority will be lost. The people will sink into misery and the nation will be doomed.[46]

Wei was found guilty of various crimes against the state, and sentenced to fifteen years in prison.

For how much longer will China be able to have more relaxed economic policies, yet persevere with political repression?

In order to encourage greater production, in recent years farmers have been allowed to sell excess food on the open market for private profit. Here watermelons are being sold in Beijing.

The Communist achievement

It is not difficult to draw up a balance sheet on the Communist achievement in China since 1949. Colin Mackerras starts with the situation when Mao and his party took over:

A modern Chinese department store in Tianjin. This city is booming and goods imported from abroad can be bought.

It is worthwhile noting the magnitude of the problems. Famine was endemic and in bad years took literally million of lives. Disease was rampant everywhere. The growing urban culture resulted in an ever widening gap between rich and poor in which hopeless squalor existed alongside great opulence. Prostitution, gambling, and vice of all kinds flourished . . . Corruption among officials was near universal . . . Chinese society was so degenerate that only radical measures could offer real hope.

It was the Communists who saw this most clearly and thought out remedial steps most realistically. While the urban intellectuals fumbled and faltered, and most of the peasants felt themselves powerless against oppression, the Communists analyzed the problems and arrived at consistent if flexible policies which could make an effective beginning in correcting China's horrifying backwardness and overwhelming poverty. This was one of the reasons why they succeeded in vanquishing the Kuomintang, and why they have continued to hold the support of the people since they came to power in 1949.[47]

Today the Chinese live longer, eat better and are in reasonable health. They are enjoying more and more the gadgets of modern technology: radios, televisions, sewing machines, watches and so forth; housing is improving, although not all Chinese can live in the kind of house shown in the picture below. Some level of education is just about universal.

What of the other side? Under Communist rule millions died in purges of anti-revolutionaries. Countless innocent and harmless people were persecuted, rejected and tortured. Basic human rights, such as the right to speak out against injustice and have a fair trial, have been ignored. Recently the birth-control issue has raised new restrictions:

Each brigade has women officials to keep an eye on the women and look out for any signs of pregnancy. There is no room for personal freedom on such an important issue! [48]

Whether one looks favorably on the Communist achievement or not, one fact is beyond dispute:

Many significant changes have occurred in world affairs during the last seventy years, such as the dissolution of the empires of the Western powers . . . the creation of the . . . United Nations, and the founding . . . of the European Community. As important as any of these, and perhaps most important, is the rebirth of a strong China. [49]

We have yet to see what China will do with its strength.

Life for peasants in China has improved greatly. Those living on communes can expect rewards for hard work. This family has recently been allotted a large and well-furnished apartment.

Leading figures

Chen Yi (Chen I) 1901–72

Like Zhou Enlai, Chen Yi spent some years in France in the 1920s before returning to China and membership in the CCP. An able commander, Chen did not go on the Long March, but remained to organize guerrilla activities in the south. He became Mayor of Shanghai after the civil war and Foreign Minister in 1958. However, as with many of the older party members, he was purged during the Cultural Revolution and died in relative obscurity.

The present leader of China, Deng Xiaoping, greets the British Prime Minister, Margaret Thatcher, in the Great Hall of the People in Beijing in 1984 before the signing of the Anglo-Chinese agreement on the future of Hong Kong after 1997.

Deng Xiaoping (Teng Hsiao-ping) 1904–

Deng's education took place in France and the USSR as well as China. During the Long March and the fighting until 1949, Deng was more involved in political organization of the Communist forces than in military matters. As a leading member of the CCP (General Secretary since 1954) he became a target of the radicals during the Cultural Revolution and was purged. In 1973, however, Deng was sufficiently back in favor to be made deputy premier of China. With the accession of Hua Guofeng in 1976, Deng was purged once more, only to reappear the next year. Since 1977 he has been a major influence in forming closer economic, political and cultural links between China and the West, and in urging liberal reforms within the country.

Hua Guofeng (Hua Kuo-fung) 1912–

After early service in the Red Army, Hua gained administrative experience in Hunan in the 1950s, but was criticized before being eclipsed somewhat during the Cultural Revolution. He survived, however, to become a leading member of the government in 1973, deputy leader in 1975, and Chairman in 1976. He purged the radical Gang of Four at once, but was soon overshadowed by Deng Xiaoping in 1978, and was demoted in 1981.

Jiang Jieshi (Chiang Kai-shek) 1887–1975

The son of a merchant, Jiang trained as a soldier in China and Japan. He supported the 1911 republican revolution of Sun Yatsen and spent six months in Moscow in 1923 studying the Red Army. By 1928 he had firm control over Sun's Guomindang party, which had divided sharply from the Communists. His increasingly corrupt regime was forced to make Chongqing its capital when the Japanese invaded in 1937. For the next twelve years, heavily supported by the United States, Jiang opposed mainly the Communists, but also the Japanese, without conspicuous success. Following the surrender of the Japanese, civil war with the Communists broke out in 1946. The GMD was destroyed and Jiang forced to flee to Taiwan (Formosa), where he remained for the rest of his life, still calling himself President of China (see picture left).

Hu Yaobang (Hu Yao-pang) 1915–

From a poor peasant background, Hu Yaobang joined the CCP in 1933, participated in the Long March and fought in the Red Army until 1949. Despite being purged twice during the Cultural Revolution, he came back into favor in the 1970s. In 1981 he was made Chairman of the Party and deputy to Deng Xiaoping, but he was dropped in 1987 following hostile reaction within the party to popular calls for liberal political reform.

Jiang Qing (Chiang Ching) 1914–

After early success as a movie actress, Jiang joined the CCP in 1937, becoming the third wife of Mao Zedong in 1939. During the Cultural Revolution she began to exert considerable influence in China, particularly over matters concerning the arts. She joined the Party's Central Committee in 1969 and was the leading member of the radical Gang of Four. She was arrested by the more moderate Hua Guofeng, tried in 1981 and sentenced to life imprisonment.

Lin Biao (Lin Piao) 1908–71

Lin Biao was trained at the same military academy (Whampoa) as Jiang Jieshi, but sided with the Communists rather than the GMD. He made a name for himself in 1948 by the brilliance of his campaign capturing Manchuria for the Communists, as a result of which he led Chinese troops in Korea (1950–53) and was created Minister of Defense in 1959. During the 1960s he was close to Mao Zedong and played an important part in the Cultural Revolution. After being declared Mao's successor in 1969, in 1971 he died in mysterious circumstances in an air crash while, it was said, fleeing to the USSR after failing to kill Mao and seize power in Beijing.

Chairman Mao Zedong inspecting a naval unit of the Chinese People's Liberation Army in 1953.

Liu Shaoqi (Liu Shao-ch'i) 1898–1974

Liu Shaoqi, like Mao Zedong, came from a peasant family. He proved an able student, however, and after a period in the USSR in the early 1920s, he became a leading member of the CCP. He took part in the Long March, became Vice-Chairman of the party in 1949 and replaced Mao as Chairman of the Republic in 1959. Reasonably practical in his views, during the Cultural Revolution he fell from favor. He was expelled from the party in 1968, and was posthumously accused of counterrevolutionary activity.

Mao Zedong (Mao Tse-tung) 1893–1976

More than anyone else, Mao was responsible for the nature and success of the Communist revolution in China. The son of a wealthy peasant, Mao first came across Marxism when working as a library assistant in Beijing University. He was present at the founding of the Chinese Communist Party in 1921 and was soon a key figure in the movement. Intellectually, his important contribution to Communist thought was emphasis upon the revolutionary importance of the peasants, not the urban proletariat, in countries such as China. He organized an abortive uprising in Hunan in 1927. Mao established soviets over large areas of Jiangxi and neighboring provinces, from where he fled on the Long March in 1934–35. From 1935 to 1947 he was based in Yanan, in northwest China. His opposition to the Japanese and his demands for land reform won him widespread support. From the flight of Jiang Jieshi in 1949 until his death in 1976, Mao dominated Chinese politics. Twice, in the Great Leap Forward of 1958 and the Cultural Revolution of 1966, he plunged the country into turmoil to ensure that revolutionary zeal did not flag. Mao was a prolific writer of political tracts, and he also wrote some poetry.

Peng Dehuai (Peng Te-huai) 1898–1974

Peng Dehuai first gained military experience under Jiang Jieshi before breaking with him and joining the Communists in 1928. Peng remained one of the leading Communist generals, playing an important part in the fighting against the GMD and the Japanese. He led China's troops in the Korean War. He was purged in 1959 for criticizing Mao's policies in the Great Leap Forward.

Stalin (Joseph Djugashvili) 1879–1953

Following Lenin's death in 1924, by clever political maneuvering Stalin became leader of the USSR by 1928. His policies of strict control by the party, collectivization of agriculture and development of the economy by Five Year Plans were the models initially followed by China in the 1950s. After Stalin's death, relations between the USSR and China began to deteriorate.

Zhou Enlai (Chou En-lai) 1898–1976

Zhou, one the intellectual leaders of the CCP, was Prime Minister from 1949 until his death. He played a crucial role in China's relations with the outside world. Educated at a missionary school, he studied in Paris (1920–21) before returning to China as a Communist leader in Shanghai and Nanchang (old spelling). As Foreign Minister between 1949 and 1958 he was primarily responsible for China's foreign policy, and he continued to maintain contact with the West during the tricky era of the Cultural Revolution, a movement of which he did not fully approve. Zhou supported the moderates in the 1970s, but he died before Mao, so was unable to see his policies through to fruition.

Zhu De (Chu-teh) 1886–1976

Unlike many Chinese Communist leaders, Zhu De came from a wealthy landowning family. After serving in the Imperial Army and under Sun Yatsen, he joined the Communists in 1925, presenting them with all his inherited wealth. His military skills were invaluable during the Long March, against the Japanese, and during the civil war of 1946–49. In 1955 Zhu was created a Marshal of the People's Republic and, despite a difficult time during the early period of the Cultural Revolution, he died a much-respected member of the CCP.

Important dates

Date	China		Date	Rest of World
1839–42	Opium Wars			
1851–64	Taiping Rebellion		1851	Great Exhibition opens in London
1900–01	Boxer Rebellion			
1911	Manchu dynasty falls.			
1912	Republic of China set up. Sun Yatsen President			
1913	Yuan Shikai President (1912–16)			
1915	Japanese invasion		1914	World War I begins
1916	Period of Warlords begins		1917	Russian Revolution
1919	GMD formed		1918	World War I ends
1921	Chinese Communist Party formed			
1923	CCP and GMD ally			
1925	Death of Sun Yatsen			
1927	Mao Zedong's "Autumn Harvest" uprising fails			
1931	Jiangxi Soviet set up under CCP Jiang Jieshi begins his campaigns against CCP Japanese occupy Manchuria		1929	World economic slump begins
1934–35	The Long March of Chinese Communists			
1935	Mao Chairman of CCP Second Sino-Japanese war begins			
1937	Second alliance of GMD and CCP		1939	World War II begins
1945	Alliance between GMD and USSR		1945	United States drops atomic bombs. Japan surrenders
1946–49	Civil war in China			End of World War II
1947	PLA takes Manchuria GMD begins to disintegrate		1948	EEC (European Economic Community) formed
1949	Jiang Jieshi flees to Taiwan People's Republic of China established		1949	NATO established
1950	Sino-Soviet alliance. Chinese troops into Korea Land Reform Law and Marriage Reform Law		1950	Korean War begins
1952	Private businesses begin to be taken over by the state			
1953	First Five Year Plan launched Cooperatives being set up		1953	Korean War ends
			1955	Warsaw Pact formed
1956	Khrushchev attacks the cult of personality Hundred Flowers Campaign		1957	Civil war in Vietnam
1958	Great Leap Forward launched Communes started (Dec.) Mao announces his intention to step down as President		1958	Khrushchev attacks communes
1959	Peng Dehuai purged. Liu Shaoqi and Deng Xiaoping in favor		1959	Khrushchev visits the United States
1960	Russian advisers leave PLA reorganized by Lin Biao Great Leap Forward over		1961	U.S. support troops enter Vietnam
1962	Fighting on border with India		1962	Cuban missile crisis

Date	China	Rest of World	
1964	*Thoughts of Chairman Mao* published	1963	L. B. Johnson becomes President of United States after the assassination of President J. F. Kennedy
1965	PLA abolishes ranks		
1966	Mao launches the Cultural Revolution Liu Shaoqi and Deng Xiaoping fall		
1967	China on verge of civil war	1967	Arab–Israeli War
1968	Red Guards sent to the countryside	1968	Student demonstrations in Paris USSR invades Czechoslovakia
1969	Border clashes with the USSR on Ussuri River Lin Biao declared Mao's successor		
1970	First satellite launched. Political stability returning	1969	U.S. astronauts land on moon
1971	Kissinger visits China Death of Lin Biao China joins United Nations		
1972	President Nixon visits China		
1973	Gang of Four gaining influence Mao's political grip in decline	1973	United States begins withdrawal from Vietnam
1975	Jiang Jieshi dies Deng Xiaoping becomes Vice-Chairman of CCP and First Vice-Premier – falls from power April 1976	1974	Watergate scandal in United States
1976	Deaths of Zhou Enlai and Mao Zedong Hua Guofeng Chairman of CCP and Premier of China Gang of Four arrested		
1977	*(July)* Deng Xiaoping reinstated as Vice-President		
1978	Treaty of Friendship and Peace with Japan Beginning of break up of communes Unofficial movement for free speech and human rights begins – "Democracy Movement"	1978	Vietnam invades Cambodia
		1978–79	Iranian revolution
1979	Normal relations with United States established Trade agreement with Britain Troops invade Vietnam's northern border	1979	Margaret Thatcher elected Prime Minister of Britain Afghanistan invaded by USSR
1980	One-Child Policy started Liberal reform of CCP attempted Trial of the Gang of Four starts		
1981	*(April)* "Democracy Movement" suppressed EEC gives China $1.5 million in food aid Hua Guofeng steps down	1981	Ronald Reagan elected President of United States
1982	Hu Yaobang becomes General Secretary of CCP United States and China agree policy toward Taiwan		
1983	Senior members of the CCP attack Deng Xiaoping's reform movement	1983	Star Wars idea begins
1984	Talks with USSR Agreement with Britain over Hong Kong Urban economic reforms begin		
1985	Attack on Deng Xiaoping's economic reforms	1985	Gorbachev leader of USSR
1986	Student protests call for freedom of speech		
1987	Hu Yaobang forced to resign		

Glossary

Arbitrary	Bound by no system of law or reason.
Bigamy	Being married to two wives or husbands at the same time.
Cadre	A group of enthusiastic CCP members.
Capitalism	An economic system that depends on the virtue of free enterprise and the right to private property and wealth.
Censorship	Altering information to suit one's own needs.
Commune	A huge farm of thousands of acres in which all land and many other articles are owned jointly by all the inhabitants.
Communism	A political and economic theory following the ideas of Karl Marx who believed in the abolition of all private property and the creation of a classless society.
Concubine	A mistress.
Confucianism	A moral system following the ideas of Confucius, which emphasized loyalty to family, peace and justice.
Conservative	Someone opposed to excessive or rapid change.
Controversial	Much argued about.
Cooperative	A group of farms sharing land and equipment.
Counterrevolutionary	The phrase used by the Communists to describe anyone who opposed them. A revolution opposed to an earlier one.
Democracy	Rule by the people or their elected representatives.
Dynasty	A ruling family.
Economy	The state of a country's finances and production.
Empire	Widespread territories and peoples under one government.
Exterminate	Destroy.
Faction	Political group.
Feudal	A society in which a few people who own all the land command obedience from all other states.
Folklore	Traditional belief.
Formosa	Taiwan. The island base of the GMD off the coast of mainland China.
Gross National Product	The total amount of wealth produced by a country.
Guerrilla	"Soldier" who engages in irregular warfare.
Imperialism	Aggressive action by a state to take over others.
Incentive	Encouragement or reward.
Infanticide	Killing unwanted babies.
Inflation	When money loses its value and prices rise faster than incomes.
Intellectuals	People interested in ideas and theories.
kWh	Kilowatt hours (a measure of electricity).
Liberalism	A philosophy that sets great store by the freedom of the individual and the rule of law.
Liberate	Set free.
Mandate	Authority.
Marxism	The ideas of Karl Marx (1818–83), a German philosopher. He claimed to have discovered the laws that govern the behavior of human society in history: societies move from feudalism, through capitalism to socialism, directed by economic forces. He held that most nineteenth-century states

were in a capitalist phase and that revolution was needed to herald in the socialist (communist) era. For its believers, Marxism explains the present and offers hope for the future.

Monogamy	Being married to one wife or husband at a time.
Monopoly	Sole control over manufacture of a product or a service.
Nationalize	The state taking over an industry or service.
Nationalism	Strong feeling for one's country.
Opulence	Wealth.
Patriotic	Supporting one's country.
Pragmatic	Taking a practical course of behavior rather than one guided by dogma.
Proletariat	The working classes.
Propaganda	Carefully selected information designed to change people's views.
Purge	Get rid of unwanted groups or individuals.
Red	Communist.
Regime	Strict system of government.
Republic	A form of government in which power is held by the people or their elected representatives.
Revolution	A complete and sometimes permanent change.
Sino	Of China.
Socialism	An economic theory that holds that the state should own all important means of the production and distribution of wealth.
Soviet	An elected council or assembly; often used after 1917 to mean anything Russian.
Stigma	Unpleasant mark.

Picture acknowledgments

The author and publishers would like to thank the following for allowing their illustrations to be reproduced in this book: Anglo-Chinese Educational Institute 15 (top), 36, 38, 42, 44, 46, 47, 49, 50, 51; BBC Hulton Picture Library 6; Camera Press 10, 21 (top), 22, 23 (top), 32, 33, 34, 37 (bottom), 41, 45; Mary Evans Picture Library 17, 18, 21 (bottom); Sally and Richard Greenhill 5; Lords Gallery cover, 29, 35, 37 (top); Peter Newark's Western Americana 9 (bottom), 13 (top), 53, 54; Photo Source 40; Popperfoto 7, 11, 12, 14, 15 (bottom), 19, 26, 27, 30, 31, 39, 43, 48; Topham 20, 23 (bottom), 24, 52; Wayland Picture Library 9 (top), 13 (bottom), 16, 28, 35. The artwork was supplied by Malcolm Walker.

Further reading

Textbooks
Guillermaz, Jacques. *The Chinese Communist Party in Power 1949–1976*. Westview Press, 1976.
Hsü, Immanuel. *The Rise of Modern China*. Oxford, 1970.

Easier Books
Bonavia, David. *The Chinese*. Penguin, 1983.
Carter, Alden R. *Modern China*. Franklin Watts, 1986.
Hacker, Jeffrey H. *The New China*. Franklin Watts, 1986.
Kolpas, Norman. *Mao*. McGraw. 1981.
Lawson, Don. *The Long March: Red China under Chairman Mao*. Crowell Jr. Books, 1983.
Macdonald, C. K. *Modern China*. Blackwell, 1985.
Poole, Frederick K. *Mao Zedong*. Franklin Watts, 1982.
Roberts, Elizabeth. *Mao Tse-tung and the Chinese Communist Revolution*. Methuen, 1970.
Snow, Edgar. *The Long Revolution*. Hutchinson, 1973.
Suyin, Han. *My House Has Two Doors*. Cape, 1980.
Williams, Simon. *China Since 1949*. Macmillan, 1985.

Scholarly Works
Chesneaux, Jean. *China: The People's Republic 1949–1976*. Pantheon, 1979.
Gelder, Stuart and Roma. *Long March to Freedom*. Hutchinson, 1962.
MacFarquhar, Roderick. *Origins of the Cultural Revolution*. Oxford, 1983.
Mackerras, Colin (ed.). *China: The Impact of Revolution*. Longman, 1976.

Original Sources
Butterfield, Fox. *China: Alive in the Bitter Sea*. Times Books, 1982.
Fau, K. H. (ed.). *The Chinese Cultural Revolution: Selected Documents*. Monthly Review, 1968.
Gittings, John. *A Chinese View of China*. BBC Publications, 1973.
Hinton, William. *Fashen: A Documentary History of Revolution in a Chinese Village*. New York, 1967.
Myrdal, Jan. *Report from a Chinese Village*. Pantheon, 1981.
Quotations from Chairman Mao Tse-tung. Foreign Language Press, Peking, 1966.
Schram, Stuart. *Chairman Mao Talks to the People*. Pantheon, 1975.
Schram, Stuart. *The Political Thought of Mao Tse-tung*. Praeger, 1963.
Spence, Jonathan D. *The Gate of Heavenly Peace*. Penguin, 1982.
Tinga Ling. *The Sun Shines Over the Sangkan River*. Foreign Language Press, Peking 1954.

Notes on sources

1 Jan Myrdal, *Report from a Chinese Village*, Pantheon, 1981.
2 Cited in Elizabeth Roberts, *Mao Tse-tung and the Chinese Communist Revolution*, Methuen, 1970.
3 From a talk between Mao Tse-tung and Louise Strong, cited in John Gittings, *A Chinese View of China*, BBC, 1973.
4 *Quotations from Chairman Mao Tse-tung*, Foreign Language Press, Peking, 1966.
5 Jan Myrdal, *op. cit.*
6 John Gittings, *op. cit.*
7 Cited in Stuart and Roma Gelder, *Long March to Freedom*, Hutchinson, 1962.
8 William Hinton, *Fashen: A Documentary History of Revolution in a Chinese Village*, New York, 1967.
9 Tinga Ling, *The Sun Shines Over the Sangkan River*, Foreign Language Press, Peking, 1954.
10 Cited in Jean Chesneaux, *China: The People's Republic, 1949–1976*, Pantheon, 1979.
11 *The Observer*, 1982.
12 "The Economy of the Chinese People's Republic" by Bruce McFarlane in Colin Mackerras (ed.), *China: The Impact of Revolution*, Longman, 1976.
13 Jacques Guillermaz, *The Chinese Communist Party in Power 1949–1976*, Westview Press, 1976.
14 Han Suyin, *My House Has Two Doors*, Cape, 1980.
15 Stuart R. Schram, *The Political Thought of Mao Tse-tung*, Praeger, 1963.
16 From the *People's Daily*, cited in C. K. Macdonald, *Modern China*, Blackwell, 1985.
17 *Quotations From Chairman Mao, op. cit.*
18 Both Mao's and Khrushchev's remarks cited in Simon Williams, *China Since 1949*, Macmillan, 1985.
19 *Quotations From Chairman Mao, op. cit.*
20 *Ibid.*
21 Jan Myrdal, *op. cit.*
22 Jacques Guillermaz, *op. cit.*
23 Roderick MacFarquhar, *Origins of the Cultural Revolution*, Vol II, Oxford, 1983.
24 From John Gittings, *op. cit.*
25 Mikhail Klochko, *Soviet Scientist in China*, 1964.
26 Jacques Guillermaz *op. cit.*
27 Stuart Schram, *Chairman Mao Talks to the People*, Pantheon, 1975.
28 K. H. Fau, ed., *The Chinese Cultural Revolution Selected Documents*, Monthly Review, 1968.
29 Edgar Snow, *The Long Revolution*, Hutchinson, 1973.
30 Cited by C. K. Macdonald, *op. cit.*
31 Han Suyin, *op. cit.*
32 Cited by C. K. Macdonald, *op. cit.*
33 Fox Butterfield, *China: Alive in the Bitter Sea*, Times Books, 1982.
34 Han Suyin, *op. cit.*
35 *Quotations from Chairman Mao, op. cit.*
36 Han Suyin, *op. cit.*
37 Jacques Guillermaz, *op. cit.*
38 Jean Chesneaux, *op. cit.*
39 Stuart Schram, *The Political Thought of Mao Tse-tung, op. cit.*
40 Edgar Snow, *op. cit.*
41 Fox Butterfield, *op. cit.*
42 Han Suyin, *op. cit.*
43 *Peking Review*, no. 12.
44 Cited in Jonathan D. Spence, *The Gate of Heavenly Peace*, Penguin, 1982.
45 Cited in Jean Chesneaux, *op. cit.*
46 Cited in Jonathan D. Spence, *op. cit.*
47 Colin Mackerras, ed., *op. cit.*
48 Cited in C. K. Macdonald, *op. cit.*
49 In the foreword to Han Suyin, *op. cit.*

Index